FOX-HUNTING

SPORT

FOX-HUNTING

PERHAPS no greater anomaly—no more palpable anachronism—exists than fox-hunting in England. Yet it has been called, and is, the " national sport." Why ? Population increases ; the island is filling up fast. The limited area unoccupied by human dwellings, machineries, and locomotive facilities of all kinds is still, in spite of bad seasons, as a rule fertile enough to supply some considerable proportion of the increasing wants of the nation. Every acre worth cultivating, let waste land reclaimers say what they will, is cultivated ; and impoverished landlords and tenants alike are less than ever able to bear the losses inflicted by broken fences, unhinged gates, and over-ridden wheat, which are the result of the inroads of constantly increasing multitudes of ignorant riders unable to distinguish seeds from squitch or turnips from tares, and which have already caused the masters of several packs of hounds to discontinue the public advertisement of their meets. Why, then, is fox-hunting, which is generally regarded as the rich man's or country squire's (by no means synonymous terms) amusement, still the popular sport of the nation ?

The reason is to be found, first, in the manly predilection inherent to our Anglo-Saxon nature for a sport into which the element of danger conspicuously enters ; and, secondly, in that it is essentially a democratic sport, wherein the favourite socialistic ideal, " The greatest happiness for the greatest number," is in some sort realised. The red coat—and not it alone, but the top-boot, or any outward and visible sign of a fox-hunter—covers a multitude of sins. The law of trespass is abolished for the day. The lands of the most exclusive aristocrat are open to the public, whether mounted or pedestrian ; and the latter have for some years past shown a keenness for and appreciation of the sport which, though it sometimes does not conduce to its

By permission of the Ackerman Galleries.

THE BICESTER HUNT, 1871

The Prince of Wales
The Spanish Ambassador

The Duke of Beaufort
The Marquis of Normanby
The Duke of Devonshire

Admiral Rous
Lord Redesdale

advancement or consummation, is not only re-markable, but also a healthy sign of its con-tinuance in the future.

But the fact is that fox-hunting—from the cream of the cream of sportsmen described by " Nimrod," to the humbler class immortalised by " Jorrocks "—spreads a vast amount of pleas-ure, satisfaction with self, and goodwill towards others over a wide surface of humanity. All classes enjoy it. The " good man across country," proud of his skill—prouder still of his reputation, and anxious, sometimes too anxious, to retain it—perhaps derives the keenest enjoy-ment of all, so long as all goes well ; but this important proviso shows that his position is not so secure, as regards happiness, as that of his humbler, less ambitious, or less proficient brethren. A slight accident, a bad start, a sudden turn of the hounds—especially if in favour of some distinguished rival on the other flank—will send him home with a bitterness of soul unknown to and incapable of realisation by those whose hopes are centred on a lesser pinnacle of fame or bliss, with whom to be absolutely first is not a *sine quâ non* for the enjoyment of a run.

But supposing all does go well. There is a burning scent, " a good fox," a good country ; he is on a good horse, and has got a good start ; then for the next twenty or thirty minutes (Elysium on earth can scarcely ever last longer) he absorbs as much happiness into his mental and physical organisation as human nature is capable of containing at one time. Such a man, so launched on his career, is difficult to catch, impossible to lead, and not very safe to follow ; but I will try to do the latter for a page or two on paper. He is riding on the left or right of the hounds (say the left for present purposes), about parallel with their centre, or a little in rear of them, if they run evenly and do not *tail*, and about fifty yards wide of them. The fields are chiefly grass, and of good size. The hounds are " racing," heads up and sterns down, with very little cry or music—indicative of a scent rarely bequeathed by modern foxes. The fences are, as a rule, strong, but not high—the " stake and bound " of the grazing countries ; but ever and anon a low but strong rail on the nearer, or the glimmer of a post on the further side, makes our friend communicate silently and mysteriously

with his horse—a fine-shouldered, strong-quar-
tered animal, almost, if not quite, thoroughbred
—as he approaches the obstacle, on the necessity
of extra care or increased exertion. It is, as the
rider knows, an " oxer," *i.e.* a strongly-laid fence,
a wide ditch, and at an interval of about three or
four feet from the former a strong single oak rail
secured between stout oak posts. Better for him
if the ditch is on the nearer and this rail on the
further side, as, if his horse jumps short, his
descending impetus will probably break it, provided it is not very strong and new, in which case
a calamity will probably occur ; but a collision
with such a rail on the nearer side may lead to
risky complications of horse and rider in the
wide ditch and fence above alluded to.

Our friend, however, has an electric or tele-
phonic system of intercourse with his horse (no
whip or spur, mind you) which secures him from
such disasters and he sails onwards smoothly—
his gallant horse taking the fences in his stride
—and now, the crowd being long ago disposed of,
and his course truly laid for two or three fields
ahead, he has leisure to inspect his company.
Right and left of him (no true sportsman ever

looks back) are some half-a-dozen good men and true going their own line ; those on the right perhaps two hundred yards wide of him, as none but a tailor will ride the line of the hounds, and they on their side allow the same lateral space or interval that he does on his. Those on his left are nearer to him, and so far have done their *devoir* gallantly in the front with himself ; but this cannot last. His is the post of advantage as well as of honour, and a slight turn to the right occurring simultaneously with the apparition of a strong " bullfinch," or grown-up unpleached thorn fence, black as Erebus, with only one weak place possible to bore through, which is luckily just in his line, turns these left hand competitors into humble followers, for at the pace hounds are going they cannot regain their parallel positions. As time goes on, similar accidents occur to the riders on the right, and these, with a fall or two and a refusal, reduce the front line to two men only, our friend on the left and one rival on the right. A ploughed field, followed by a grass one, ridge-and-furrow and uphill, makes our friend take a pull at his horse, for the ridges are " against " or across him ; they are high and old-fashioned, and covered with molehills, while the furrows are very deep and " sticky," causing even our skilled friend to roll about rather like a ship at sea, and less practised riders to broach-to altogether. As he labours across this trying ground, " hugging the wind," so to speak, as closely as he can, keeping the sails of his equine craft just full and no more—with a tight hold of his head, his anxious eye earnestly scans the sky line, where looms out an obstacle, the most formidable yet encountered—a strong staken-bound fence *leaning towards him*, which he instinctively knows to be garnished on the other side with a very wide ditch, whether or not further provided with an ox-rail beyond that, he cannot tell. What he sees is enough—considering the ground he has just traversed, and that he must go at the fence uphill —to make him wish himself safe over. However, with a sense of relief, he sees a gleam of daylight in it, which he at first half hopes is a gap, but which turns out to be a good stiff bit of timber nailed between two ash trees. It is strong and high, but lower than the fence ; the " take off " is good, and there is apparently no width of ditch beyond. So, thanking his stars or favourite saint

that " timber " is his horse's special accomplish-
ment, he " goes for it." It don't improve on
acquaintance. Now is the time for hands. Often
—oh, how often !—have hands saved the head or
the neck ! and fortunately his are faultless. Without hurry, just restraining his impatience (he has
the eagerness of youth), yet leaving him much to
himself, he puts his horse at it in a steady hand
canter, dropping his hand at the instant the sen-
sible beast takes off to an inch in the right place,
and he is safe over without even a rap.

A glorious sea of grass is now before him.

Quocunque adspicias, nihil est nisi *gramen* et aër !

A smooth and gradual slope with comparatively
small fences leads down to the conventional line
of willows which foreshadows the inevitable
brook, without which neither in fact nor story can
a good run with hounds occur. Now it is that our
hero shows himself a consummate master of his
art. The ploughed and ridge-and-furrow fields,
above alluded to, followed by the extra exertion
of the timber jump at the top of the hill, have
rather taken the " puff " out of his gallant young
horse, and besides, from the same causes the

hounds by this time have got rather the better of him. In short, they are a good field ahead of him, and going as fast as ever. This would the eager and excitable novice—ay, not only he, but some who ought to know better—think the right time to recover the lost ground, and " put the steam on " down the hill. O fool ! Does the engine-driver " put the steam on " at the top of Shap Fell ? He shuts it off—saves it ; the incline does the work for him without it. Our friend does the same ; pulls his horse together, and for some distance goes no faster than the natural stride of his horse takes him down the hill. Consequently the lungs, with nothing to do, refill with air and the horse is himself again ; whereas, if he had been hurried just at that moment, he would have " gone to pieces " in two fields. Half a mile or so further on, having by increase of pace and careful observation of the leading hounds, resulting in judicious nicks, recovered his position on the flank of the pack, he finds himself approaching the brook. He may know it to be a big place, or be ignorant of its proportions ; but, in either case, his tactics are the same. He picks out a spot where no broken banks appear, and the grass is visible on the other side, and where, if any, there may be a stunted bush or two on his side of it ; there he knows the bank is sound, for there is nothing more depressing than what may happen, though mounted on the best water jumper in your stable, to find yourself and him, through the breaking down of a treacherous undermined bank in the very act of jumping the brook sub- siding quietly into the water. The bush at least secures him from such a fate. About one hun- dred yards from the place he " steadies " his horse almost to a hand canter till within half a dozen strides of the brook, when he sits down in his saddle, and lets him go at it full speed. The gallant beast knows what this means, and also by cocking his ears, snatching at the bridle, and snorting impatiently, shows his master that he is aware of what is before him. Through the com- bination of his own accurate judgment and his master's fine handling, he takes off exactly at the right distance, describes an entrancing parabola in the air, communicating to his rider as near an approach to the sensation of flying as mortal man can experience, and lands with a foot to spare on the other side of the most dreaded and historically

By permission of the Embleton Galleries.

"What! four of us only? are these the survivors,
    Of all that rode gaily from Ranksboro' Ridge,
I hear the faint splash of a few hardy divers,
    The rest are in hopeless research of a bridge."

disastrous impediment in the whole country—a good eighteen feet of open water.

And now, perhaps, our friend realises the full measure of his condensed happiness, not un-mixed with selfishness ; as perhaps he would own, while he gallops along the flat meadow, not forgetting to pat his horse, especially as he hears a faint " swish " from the water, already one hun-dred yards in his rear ; the result, as he knows, of the total immersion of his nearest follower, which as he also knows, will probably bar the way to many more, for a " brook with a man in it " is a frightful example, an objectionable and fear-inspir-ing spectacle to men and horses alike, and there is not a bridge for miles. As for proffering assis-tance, I fear it never enters his head. He don't know who it is, and mortal and imminent peril on the part of a dear friend would alone induce him to forego the advantage of his present position, and he knows there are plenty behind too glad of the opportunity, as occasionally with soldiers in a battle, of retiring from the fray in aid of a disabled comrade. So he sails on in glory, the hounds running, if anything, straighter and faster than ever. That very morning, perchance, he was full of care, worried by letters from lawyers and stewards, duns, announcements of farms thrown upon his hands ; and, if an M.P., of a certain contest at the coming election. Where are all these now ? Ask of the winds ! They are vanished. His whole system is steeped in delight; there is not space in it for the absorption of another sensation. Talk of opium ? of hashish ? they cannot supply such voluptuous entrancement as a run like this !

" Taking stock " again of his company, he is rather glad to see (for he is not an utterly selfish fellow) that the man on the right has also got safely over the big brook, and is going well ; but there is absolutely no one else in sight. It is clear that unless a " check " of some duration occurs, or the scent should die away, or the fox should deviate from his hitherto straight course, these two cannot be overtaken, or even approached. No such calamity—for in this case it *would* be a calamity—takes place ; and the hounds, now evincing that peculiar savage eagerness which denotes the vindictive mood known as " running for blood," hold on their way across a splendid grass country for some two miles further with diminished speed. Then an excited rustic is seen waving his hat as he runs to open a gate for our friend on the left exclaiming, as the latter gallops through with hurried but sincere thanks, " He's close afore 'em : they'll have him soon ! " And sure enough, a field or two further the sight of a dark brown object slowly toiling up a long pasture-field by the side of a high straggling thorn fence causes our now beaming rider to rise in his stirrups and shout, for the information and encouragement of his companion on the right, " Yonder he goes ! " The hounds, though apparently too intent on their work to notice this ejaculation, seem nevertheless to somewhat appreciate its import, for their leaders appear to press forward with a panting, bloodshot impatience ominous of the end. Yet a few more fields, and over the crown of the hill the dark brown object is to be seen in slow rolling progression close before them. And now " from scent to view," with a final crash of hound-clamour followed by dead silence, as fox and hounds together involve themselves in a confused entangled ball or heap in the middle of a splendid pasture only two fields from the wood which had been the fox's point from the first ; and many a violated henroost and widowed gander is avenged!

Our friend is off his horse in an instant, and leaving him with outstretched legs and quivering tail (no fear of his running away—he had been jumping the last few fences rather " short "), is soon occupied in laying about the hounds' backs with his whip gently and judiciously (it don't do for a stranger to be too energetic or disciplinarian on these rare occasions), and with the help of his friend, who arrives only an instant later, and acts with similar promptitude and judgment, succeeds in clearing a small ring round the dead fox. " Whoohoop ! " they both shout alternately, but rather breathlessly, as Ravager and Ruthless make occasional recaptures of the fox, requiring strong coercive measures before they yield possession. " Who has a knife ? " They can hardly hear themselves speak ; and a fumbling in the pocket, rather than the voice, conveys the inquiry. Our friend has ; and placing his foot on the fox's neck contrives to cut off the brush pretty artistically. He hands it to his companion, and wisely deciding to make no post-mortem surgical efforts on the head,

holds the stiff corpse aloft for one moment only—
the hounds are bounding and snapping, and the
situation is getting serious—and hurls it with a
final " Whoohoop ! " and " Tear him ! " which
latter exhortation is instantly and literally followed, among the now absolutely uncontrollable
canine mob. And now both, rather happy to find
themselves unbitten, form themselves on the spot,
and deservedly, into a small Mutual Admiration
Society, for they are the sole survivors out of perhaps three hundred people, and ecstatically com-
pare notes on this long-to-be-remembered run.
Meanwhile the huntsman first, and the rest of the
field by degrees and at long intervals, come
straggling up from remote bridges and roads. It
has not been a run favourable to the " point
rider," who sometimes arrives at the " point "
before the fox himself, for it has been quite
straight, measuring on the map six miles from
point to point, and the time, from the " holloa
away " to the kill, exactly thirty minutes.

And here, leaving our two friends to receive the
congratulations (not all of them quite sincere) of
an admiring and envious field, and to apologise to
the huntsman for the hurried obsequies of the

fox, whereby his brush and head—the latter still contended for by some of the more insatiable hounds, and a half-gnawed pad or two—are by this time the only evidence of his past existence, I will leave the record of deeds of high renown, and, having shown the extreme of delight attainable by the first-class men or senior wranglers of fox-hunting, proceed to demonstrate how happiness likewise attends those who don't go in for honours—who are only too happy with a " pass," and what endless sources of joy the hunting-field supplies to all classes of riders. In short, to paraphrase a line of Pope, to

See some strange comfort every sort supply.

From the very first I will go to the very last ; and among these, strange to say, the very hardest riding often occurs. When I have found myself, as I often have—and as may happen through combinations of circumstances to the best of us— among the very last in a gallop, I have observed a touching spectacle. Men, miles in the rear, seeing nothing of the hounds, caring nothing for the hounds, riding possibly in an exactly opposite direction to the hounds, yet with firm determination in their faces, racing at the fences, crossing each other, jostling and cramming in gateways and gaps. These men, I say, are enjoying themselves after their manner, as thoroughly as the front rank. These men neither give nor take quarter, but ride over and are ridden over with equal complacency, without a hound in sight or apparent cause for their violent exertions and daring enterprises. For though the post of honour may be in front, the post of danger is in the *mêlée* of the rear. Honour to the brave, then, here as in the front. Here, as in the front, there is perfect equality. Here, also, as everywhere in the field, there are the self-assertion, independence, communistic contempt for private property, and complete freedom of action, which constitute the main charm of the sport. No questions of precedence here ; every man is free to ride where he likes. The chimney sweep can go before the duke, and very often does so. Here, as in the front, precedence at a fence, gap, or gate is settled on the lines of the

Good old plan,
That he should take who has the power,
And he should keep who can.

The late Mr. Surtees, whose " Jurrocks," " Sponge," and " Facey Romford " are immortal characters, used to say that the tail of a run, where he himself almost always rode, was the place for sport ; that, in addition to the ludicrous incidents there occurring so frequently for his entertainment, human nature could be studied with the greatest advantage from that position. And indeed he was right, for there is more to study from. And with what varieties. The half hard, the wholly soft, the turbulent, the quiescent, the practical, the geographical and the political or digestion-seeking rider, these men are to be studied from the rear, because few of them are ever seen in front ; and nevertheless they return to their homes justified fully as much in their own opinion as he who has in point of fact, and undoubtedly, " had the best of it " all through the run. This merciful arrangement or dispensation makes every rider contented and happy in his own way.

Among these is to be found the " hard " rider who devotes his attention entirely to fences, and never looks at the hounds at all. Consequently, he never sees a run, but is quite satisfied if he jumps a certain number of large fences, and gets a corresponding average of falls in the day. The late Lord Alvanley seeing one of these gentlemen riding furiously at a fence not in the direction of the hounds, shouted to him " Hi ! hi ! " and when the surprised and somewhat indignant sportsman stopped his horse, and turned to know what was the matter, pointed to another part of the fence and added calmly, " There's a much bigger place here ! " This man, too, thoroughly enjoys himself, gets plenty of exercise, and at the same time provides good means of livelihood for the local surgeon. Then there is the violent rider, who would be annoyed if he knew that he was generally called the " Squirter," who gallops, but doesn't jump ; though from his severely cut order of clothing, general horsiness of appearance, and energetic behaviour in the saddle, he is apt to impose on those who don't know how quiescent and harmless the first fence will immediately render him. His favourite field of operations is a muddy lane, where he gallops past with squared elbows and defiant aspect, scattering more mud behind him than any one horse and man ever before projected or cast back upon an astonished and angered public. Through the gate, if any, at the end he crams his way, regardless alike of such expressions as " Take care ! " " Where are you coming to ? "—an absurd question, decidedly, the object being evident—and also very properly disregarding and treating with utter contempt the man (always to be found in a gateway) who says " There is no hurry ! " a gratuitous falsehood, as his own conduct sufficiently proves. In the open field beyond he rushes like a whirlwind past any one who may be in front, and, so long as gates or only small gaps are in his line, pursues a triumphant course. But he has no root, and in time of temptation is apt to fall away : that is, the moment a fence of the slightest magnitude presents itself. Then he fades away—disappears, and is no more seen ; yet he, like the ephemera, has had his day, though a short one, and returns to his well-earned rest contented and happy.

Then there is a character for whom I have always had a sincere respect and sympathy—the " hard funker." Than he no man has a more cruel lot. He is the victim of a reputation. On some occasion his horse ran away with him, or some combination of circumstances occurred, resulting in his " going " brilliantly in a run, or being carried safely over some impossible place which, though he subsequently, like Mr. Winkle in his duel, had presence of mind enough to speak of and treat as nothing out of the way, and to have jumped which was to him an ordinary occurrence, he could not in any unguarded moment contemplate, allude to, or even think of without shuddering. By nature nervous and timid—weaknesses reacted upon as a sort of anti-dote by a love of notoriety and a secret craving for admiration and applause—this heavy calamity had occurred to him, from which he could never shake himself free.

> The burden of an honour
> Unto which he was not born,

clung to him wheresoever he went. Greatness was thrust upon him. He must ride ; it was ex-pected from him. *Noblesse oblige !* he hates it, but he must do it. It embitters his life, but he dare not sacrifice the reputation. The eyes of Europe are upon him, as he thinks ; and so, though in mortal fear during the most part of every hunting day, he endures it. He suffers, and is strong. Each day requires from him some feat of daring for the edification of the field ; and he does it, usually executing it in sight of the whole field, when hounds are running slowly, charging some big fence, which there is no real necessity for jumping, at full speed, and shutting his eyes as he goes over. The county analyst, if called upon to examine the contents of the various flasks carried by the field, would pronounce this gentleman's sherry or brandy to be less diluted with water than any one else's. Honour to him ! If you feel no fear, what credit to ride boldly ? But if you really " funk," and ride boldly, this is to be brave indeed.

Then among the more passive class of riders comes the man who goes in entirely for " a sporting get-up," especially for a faultless boot, which is generally regarded as a sure indication of riding power. The old Sir Richard Sutton, when asked, during his mastership of the Quorn Hounds, whether So-and-so, recently arrived from the country, could ride, replied : " I don't know—I have not seen him go ; but I should think he could, for he *hangs a good boot.*" To arrive, however, at this rarely attained perfection of sporting exterior, I grieve to say that an almost total absence of calf is indispensable ; but with this physical advantage in his favour, if he can otherwise " dress up to it," very little more is required from him. He expends all his energies on his " get-up," and when he is " got-up " he is done and exhausted for the day, and is seldom seen out of a trot or a lane. Then there is the man " who can tell you all about it." He will describe the whole run, with fervent and florid descriptions of this awkward fence, or that wide brook, not positively asserting, but leaving you to infer, that he was in the front rank all the way ; but somehow no one else will have ever seen him in any part of the run. This rider is gifted with a vivid imagination and vast powers of invention, and, as a rule, never leaves the road. Then there is the politician who button-holes you at every possible opportunity on the subject of the Affirmation Bill, extracting from you probably, as your attention is most likely not intent on this matter just then, some " oaths " not required by the statute. Then there is, finally, the honest man who comes out, without disguise or pretence, solely for the benefit of his digestion ; who never intends to jump, and never does jump.

All these varied classes are happy, and not a few of them go home under the firm impression that they have distinguished themselves ; and some even comfort themselves with the reflection that they have " cut down " certain persons, who are probably quite unaware of this operation having been performed upon them, or may possibly be of opinion that they themselves have performed it on the very individuals who are thus rejoicing in this reversed belief.

With all this there is throughout these varied classes of riders, although occasional bickerings may arise, a general tone of good humour and tolerance rarely to be found in other congregations of mankind. Landlords and tenant farmers —whose natural relation to each other has recently been described by political agitators (with their usual accuracy) as one of mutual coldness, distrust, and antagonism—here meet with smiling countenances and jovial greetings, and the only question of " tenant right " here is the right of the tenant to ride over his landlord, or of the landlord to take a similar liberty with his tenant. Rivals in business, opponents in politics, debtors and creditors—all by common consent seem to wipe off old scores, and, for the day at least, to be at peace and charity with their neighbours.

One man only may perhaps be sometimes excluded from the benefits arising out of this approximation to the millennium, and he, to whom I have not yet alluded, is the most important of all—the master. No position, except perhaps a member of Parliament's, entails so much hard work, accompanied with so little thanks, as that of a master of fox-hounds. A " fierce light," inseparable from his semi-regality, beats on him ; his every act is scrutinised and discussed by eyes and tongues ever ready to mark and proclaim what is done amiss. Very difficult is it for him to do right. There are many people to please, and often what pleases one offends another. Anything going wrong, any small annoyance, arriving too late at the meet, getting a bad start, drawing away from, and not towards, the grumbler's home (and grumblers, like the poor, must always be among us)—all these things are apt to be somehow visited on the unhappy master.

> Upon the King ! let us our lives—our souls,
> Our debts, . . . our sins, lay on the King !

Then there is the anxiety for his hounds' safety among wild riders and kicking three-year olds. He knows each hound, and has a special affection for some, which makes him in gateways or narrow passes, as they thread their way among the horses' feet, shudder to his inmost core. Sir Richard Sutton was once overheard, when arriving at the meet, putting the following questions to his second-horse man : " Many people out ? " " A great many, Sir Richard." " Ugh ! Is Colonel F. out ? " " Yes, Sir Richard." " Ugh, ugh ! Is Mr. B. out ? " " Yes, Sir Richard." " Ugh, ugh, ugh ! Then couple up ' Valiant ' and ' Dauntless,' and send them both home *in the brougham !* "

This same master in my hearing called aside at one of his meets a gentleman, who was supposed by him to be not very particular as to how near he rode to the hounds, and, pointing out one particular hound, said : " Please kindly take notice of

"Then steady, my young one, my place I've selected,
　　Above the dwarf willow 'tis sound I'll be bail,
With your muscular quarters beneath you collected,
　　Prepare for a rush like the limited mail."

that hound. He is the most valuable animal in the pack, and I would not have him ridden over for anything." The gentleman promptly and courteously replied : " I would do anything to oblige you, Sir Richard ; but I have a shocking bad memory for hounds, and *I'm afraid he will have to take his chance with the rest !* " All these things are agonising to a master, and other anxieties perplex him. He knows how much of his sport depends on the good will of the tenant farmers, and he sees with pain rails needlessly broken, crops needlessly ridden over, gates unhinged or left open, perhaps fronting a road along which the liberated cattle or horses may stray for miles, giving their angry proprietors possibly days of trouble to recover them. Second-horsemen too are often careless in this respect. But I must here remark as to the tenant farmers, that, as a rule, their tolerance is beyond all praise, especially when, as unfortunately is the case in many countries, the mischievous trespassers above alluded to have no connection with the county or hunt, do not subscribe to the hounds, or spend a shilling directly or indirectly in the neighbourhood.

Time was when the oats, the straw, and the hay were bought and consumed by the stranger in the land, who thus brought some advantage to the farmer, and in other matters to the small trader. But now he arrives by train and so departs leaving broken fences and damaged crops as the only trace of his visit. These are the evils which may lead to the decadence of fox-hunting. But Mr. Oakeley, master of the Atherstone, an especially and deservedly popular man, it is true, had a magnificent proof of an opposite conclusion the other day, when over a thousand tenant farmers, on the bare rumour of the hounds being given up, got up, and signed in a few days, a testimonial or memorial to beg him to continue them, and pledging themselves to do all they could to promote the sport in every way. This is the bright side of a " master's " life.

But not to all is it given to bask in such sunshine. Earnest labour is required to attain this or any other success. And the following rules, I believe, always guided Mr. Oakeley's conduct as a master :

1. To buy his horses as much as possible from the farmers themselves—not from dealers.

2. To buy his forage in the country.

3. To keep stallions for use of farmers at a low fee, and to give prizes for young horses bred in the district. (In both these objects many are of opinion that the master ought to be helped by the State, as nothing would encourage the breeding of horses so much, or at such small cost.)

4. To give prizes, and create rivalry as to the " walked " puppies, by asking the farmers over to see them when they returned to headquarters, and giving them luncheon.

5. To draw all coverts in their turn, and not to cut up any particular portion unduly because it may be a better country with more favourite coverts.

Lastly. To get farmers to act for themselves as much as possible in the management of poultry claims, etc., which they will then have a pride in keeping low. And above all, ever to recognise and acknowledge that tenant farmers have, to say the least, an equal voice with the landowners as to the general management of the hunting.

But I have done. I have shown, I hope, that, on the whole, fox-hunting brings happiness to all —the fox, when killed or hard run excepted—but

I cannot go into the larger question of humanitarian sentiment ; he is often *not* killed ; and till he is, leads a jovial life, feasting on the best, and thief, villain, and murderer as he is, protected even by the ruthless gamekeeper. In return for this his day of atonement must come. But for the sport, he would not have existed ; and when he dies gallantly in the open, as in the run above depicted, his sufferings are short. I myself like not the last scene of some hunts, when, his limbs having failed him, the poor fox is driven to depend on the resources of his vulpine brain alone. Often have I turned aside, declining to witness the little stratagems of his then piteous cunning ; nay, more, I confess, when I alone have come across the hiding-place of a " beaten fox," and he has, so to speak, confided his secret to me with his upturned and indescribably appealing eye, it has been sacred with me ; I have retired softly, and rejoiced with huge joy when the huntsman at last called away his baffled pack.

Altogether, I maintain that, with such exceptions, at small cost of animal suffering, great enjoyment is compassed by all. There are miseries of course even out hunting ; there are rainy days, bad scenting days and inconvenient mounts. The celebrated Jem Mason, a splendid rider and quaint compounder of expressions, used to say that the height of human misery was to be out hunting on a " ewe-necked horse, galloping over a molehilly field, down hill, with bad shoulders, a snaffle bridle, one foot out of the stirrup, and a fly in your eye." But he dealt in figurative extremes. He replied to some one who asked him as to the nature of a big-looking fence in front : "Certain death on this side, my lord, and eternal misery on the other ! " Such sorrows as these are not much to balance against the weight of happiness in the other scale. So I myself in my old age still preserve the follies of my youth, and counsel others to do the same. " Laugh and be fat," says some modern advertisement. " Hunt and be happy," say I still. But who shall pierce the veil of the future ? As with the individual, so I think it is with nations. They too, when they grow old, should preserve, or at least, not too remorselessly extinguish, their follies. I fear lest in grasping at the shadow of national perfection we only attain the reality of a saturnalia of prigs—an apotheosis of claptrap. Legislation has performed such

queer antics lately that the angels must be begin-
ning to weep. And ugly visions sometimes haunt
me of a time coming, which shall be a good time
to no man, at least to no Englishman, when an
impossible standard of pseudo-philanthropy and
humanitarian morality shall be attempted ; when
the butcher shall lie down with the lamb, the
alderman with the turtle, and the oyster shall not
be eaten without anæsthetics ; when nature itself
shall be under the eye of the police, and detectives
watch the stoat's pursuit of the rabbit and keep
guard over spiders' webs ; when all property
(and not in land alone, my advanced friend !) save
that of hardware magnates, who have made a
monopoly and called it peace, shall be confiscated
as an " unearned increment " to the State ; when
we have by legislative enactment forbidden the
prevention and sanctioned the admission of loath-
some diseases, and anti-fox-hunting may be as
loud a cry as anti-vaccination ; when there is a
Parliament on College Green ; when the " lan-
guishing nobleman " of Dartmoor is free, and
repossessed of his broad acres, which, in his case
alone, because they so clearly belong to some one
else, shall escape confiscation ; when, as a final

climax to our national madness, we have employed science to dig a hole under the sea, and, by connecting us with the Continent, deprive us of the grand advantage which nature has given us, and which has conferred on us centuries of envied stability, while thrones were rocking and constitutions sinking all around us ; when, having already passed laws not only to prohibit our children being educated with the knowledge and fear of God before their eyes, but even to forbid His very name to be mentioned in our schools, we deliberately and scornfully abandon our ancient religion and admit proclaimed infidelity and public blasphemy to the sanction, recognition, and approval of Parliament ;—then indeed we need not wonder if we lose not only our national sports, but our national existence ; and if Divine Providence, giving practical effect to the old quotation,

Quos Deus vult perdere prius dementat,

allows England, after passing through the phases of insanity which she has already begun to display, to be blotted out from the nations of the world.